# Wh

# Mount Everest?

# Where Is Mount Everest?

by Nico Medina

illustrated by John Hinderliter

Grosset & Dunlap
An Imprint of Penguin Group (USA) LLC

For Aunt Diane—NM

For Rose and Ruby, who won't stop
asking questions. Keep it up—JH

GROSSET & DUNLAP
Published by the Penguin Group
Penguin Group (USA) LLC, 375 Hudson Street, New York, New York 10014, USA

USA | Canada | UK | Ireland | Australia | New Zealand | India | South Africa | China

penguin.com
A Penguin Random House Company

*Library of Congress Cataloging-in-Publication Data is available.*

ISBN 978-0-448-48408-2                    10 9 8 7 6 5 4 3 2 1

# Contents

Mount Everest

# Where Is Mount Everest?

April 18, 2014, was the deadliest day in the history of Mount Everest.

Standing on the border between Nepal and China, this mammoth mountain rises more than 29,000 feet—nearly five and a half miles—into the sky. It is the highest point on earth. More than four thousand people have reached the top of Everest. Hundreds more have died trying.

Early that morning in 2014, around fifty men were on the mountain. Suddenly, a block of ice the size of a house broke off a cliff. It cracked into truck-size pieces. The ice chunks tumbled down the mountainside, instantly killing those in its path. For days, people dug in the snow and ice, hoping to find survivors. But in the end, sixteen men lost their lives.

Most of the men on the mountain that day were Sherpas, the native people of the area. To the Sherpas, Everest is known as *Chomolungma*. That means "Mother Goddess of the World." They revere and respect her. On that fateful Friday morning, Chomolungma reminded them—and the world—of the mountain's savage power.

A Sherpa village

Every year, hundreds of people from around the world try to reach the summit of Mount Everest. Many of these adventure-seekers pay Sherpas to be their guides. This is how a lot of Sherpas make a living.

But climbing Everest can be a dangerous business.

Avalanches—fast-moving walls of snow—are common.

Violent snowstorms appear out of nowhere.

Hurricane-force winds make the subzero temperatures feel even colder.

The frozen ground beneath your feet can split open, revealing cracks more than a hundred feet deep.

Near the summit, there is an area known as the Death Zone. The air is so thin—so lacking in oxygen—that you can hardly breathe.

No life exists at the top of Everest. Humans who reach the top must turn around and climb back down right away. If not, they face certain death. But despite these many dangers, climbers come back year after year.

It's natural to wonder why someone would take such risk for a chance to stand on top of a mountain. Different people have different reasons. But when one mountaineer was asked why he wished to climb Mount Everest, his answer was simple: "Because it's there."

# The Empire State Building versus Everest

Everyone knows that Mount Everest is tall. But just how tall *is* 29,000 feet? If turned on its side, it would be the length of almost one hundred football fields! Or 175 laps in an Olympic-size pool! Mount Everest is nearly five times taller than the Grand Canyon is deep!

Another way to understand the height of Everest is to think about the Empire State Building in New York City. For over forty years, it was the tallest building in the whole world. Now imagine stacking one Empire State Building on top of another. You would have to stack twenty of them to reach the height of Mount Everest.

# CHAPTER 1
## Birth of a Mountain

The Himalayan mountain range—home to Mount Everest—stretches more than 1,500 miles across Asia. It runs from Pakistan through Bhutan. The Himalayas rise higher than any other mountains in the world—by a long shot. More than one hundred Himalayan peaks are over

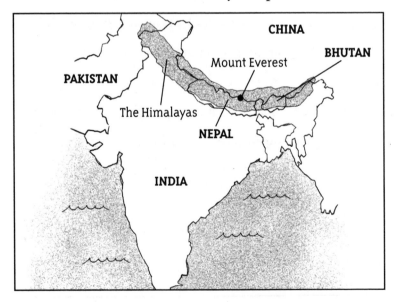

24,000 feet above sea level. Mount Aconcagua in South America is the tallest mountain outside Asia. It stands at 22,841 feet. That is more than a *mile* shorter than Mount Everest.

Despite Everest's height, fossils of prehistoric sea creatures can be found near the top. That's because millions of years ago, the rocks that would later become the Himalayas lay at the bottom of an ancient ocean!

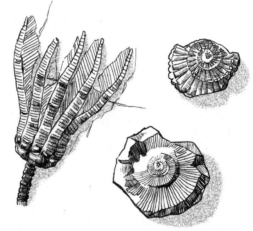

Plate tectonics—the movement of large sections of the Earth's crust and upper mantle—gave rise to these great mountains.

# Earth's Layers

Our planet is made of three layers: the crust, the mantle, and the core. Picture the Earth like a peach— the skin is the crust, the fruity flesh is the mantle, and the pit, or seed, is the core.

We live on the Earth's crust. It is much thinner than the other two layers. Crust under the oceans is around six miles thick. The crust on dry land can be

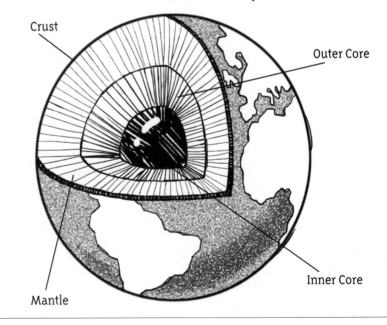

Crust

Outer Core

Inner Core

Mantle

up to thirty-five miles thick. (Both the mantle and the core are around two thousand miles thick.)

The rocks in the upper mantle (closest to the crust) are cool and brittle. When they break, earthquakes can occur. The crust and the upper mantle are constantly in motion. But it's very *slow* motion—they move just a couple of inches a year.

The core of the Earth is at the center of the planet, past the crust and the mantle. Temperatures here can reach more than ten thousand degrees Fahrenheit—as hot as the surface of the sun!

Three hundred million years ago, there was no Asia or Africa, no North or South America. This is because all the land on Earth was part of a single "supercontinent" that we now call Pangaea (say: pan-JEE-uh).

Pangaea

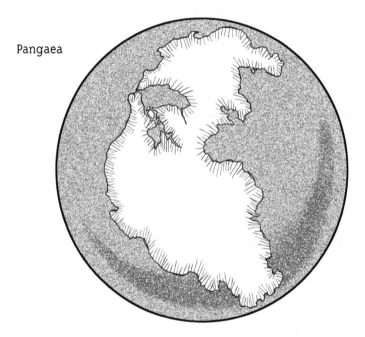

About two hundred million years ago, Pangaea began to break apart. When this happened, India became an island.

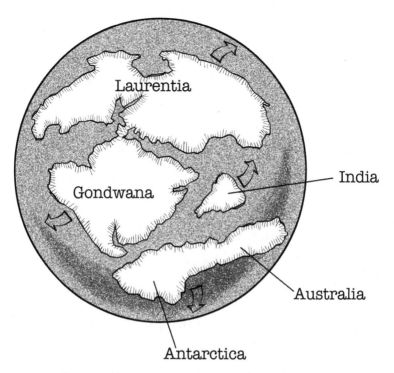

Laurentia

Gondwana

India

Australia

Antarctica

Eighty million years ago—when dinosaurs still walked the earth—India began to drift toward what is now Asia. India was moving quickly, about four inches per year. That is more than twice as fast as human fingernails grow!

Year by year, the sea between the two landmasses grew smaller and smaller. After thirty million years, the sea had disappeared altogether, and India crashed into Asia. The seafloor folded up on itself. It began to push toward the sky. In another twenty-five million years, the Himalayas were born.

When the rock could fold no further, it broke and sunk down toward the Earth's mantle. Here, at temperatures of more than four thousand degrees, the rock melted and flowed away. This made room for more rock to sink and melt. As melted rock floated back toward the surface, it cooled and hardened. This put pressure on the young mountains above it, pushing them even higher.

This mountain-building process continues today. India continues to push under Asia, and Mount Everest grows a little bit every year.

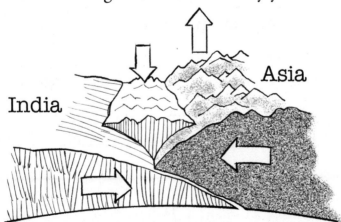

# Earthquakes

Earthquakes occur where two large pieces of the Earth's crust—or *plates*—meet. These plates are always moving, their edges rubbing against each other. Sometimes, the plates' edges get stuck. As the plates continue to push into each other with nowhere to go, pressure builds up. Eventually, the plates become unstuck, and can move again. At that point, all the pressure that had built up as the plates pushed into each other gets released. The result is an earthquake. Earthquakes are common in the Himalayas.

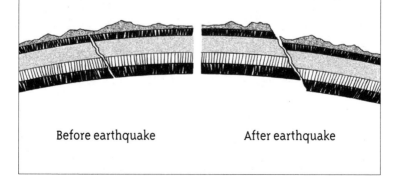

Before earthquake                    After earthquake

*Himalaya* means "snow home" in the ancient Indian language of Sanskrit. The Himalayas are so tall, they are covered in snow and glaciers year-round. Mount Everest is sometimes called the "Third Pole." Only the North and South Poles contain more snow than the Himalayas.

When Himalayan snow melts, it feeds great rivers—the Ganges, Indus, Yangtze, Mekong, and others. From Afghanistan to Thailand, these rivers provide water for more than one billion people—one out of every five people in the world!

The Himalayas also affect the weather in the region.

Every summer, warm, wet winds blow north from the Indian Ocean. When these winds reach the Himalayas, they rise upward, forming rain clouds. The rains fall hard over India in the summer months, watering crops and swelling rivers. High in the mountains, the rain falls as snow and ice. This weather pattern is known as the monsoon. Without the Himalayas to block them, the warm winds would simply blow into China and Russia, and the monsoon rains would not fall.

Cherrapunji is a town in India 325 miles east of Mount Everest. It is often said to be the wettest

place on earth. Every year it gets more than 450 inches of rainfall. That's more than ten times the amount of rain that falls in Seattle, Washington—a city known for rainy days!

The mountains also keep India warm, blocking out cold Arctic winds from the north.

Indeed, people in many areas across Asia—from the highlands of Nepal to the jungles of Myanmar—depend on these magnificent mountains for life itself.

## CHAPTER 2
## The People of Everest

People have lived in the Himalayas for thousands of years. But the Khumbu (say: KOOM-boo) Valley, the high and rugged area surrounding Mount Everest, was settled only five hundred years ago by the Sherpa people. They came from south-central Tibet. That's a region in China on the north side of the Himalayas.

Tibetan people knew about the Khumbu Valley for years before it was settled. A few visited the beautiful wilderness to be at peace with their thoughts. But it was not until 1533 that the first settlers—a group of between twenty-five and fifty Sherpas on horseback—arrived in Khumbu, and stayed.

They were hunter-gatherers, foraging for wild mushrooms and bamboo shoots to eat. They lived in caves and bamboo huts. Eventually villages were built, and terraces were carved out of the mountainsides for planting wheat and barley.

As they still do to this day, the Sherpas raised long-haired oxen called yaks. Yaks have small hooves with sharp edges that give them control in difficult and slippery terrain, much like a mountaineer's climbing tools. The Sherpas use them to carry heavy loads. Meat, milk, butter, wool, leather, and fertilizer come from yaks.

Because of the extremely rough land, there are no roads in the Khumbu Valley. Even the use of wagons and wheelbarrows is difficult. So yaks are still used for travel. Along steep and narrow mountain paths, the yaks climb the nineteen-thousand-foot-high Nangpa Pass loaded down with Sherpa goods, and return with salt from Tibet.

Whatever loads are not carried by yaks are carried by the Sherpas themselves. Known for their strength, Sherpa guides can carry loads of up to one hundred pounds on their backs.

The religion of the Sherpa people is a form of Buddhism in which many deities, or gods and goddesses, exist. The Sherpas also believe in demons. Their gods can protect people from these demons. In return, the gods must be respected and provided with offerings.

# Buddhism

Buddhism is a religion practiced by more than three hundred million people worldwide. It began roughly 2,500 years ago, when a prince named Siddhartha Gautama (say: Si-DAR-tuh GOW-tuh-muh) was born.

Prince Siddhartha lived a comfortable life. But as he grew up, Siddhartha realized that a life of luxury was not the key to happiness. So what was? For years, he thought about this. At the age of thirty-five, he discovered the answers. That was the moment he became the Buddha, or "the enlightened one." To be enlightened means to find true meaning inside yourself.

To find happiness, a person needed to lead a life

of kindness and to always think of others. A person should not want more things than are really needed, for this only leads to unhappiness. Siddhartha taught others what he had learned until he died around the age of eighty.

The Buddha is often depicted in art and statues as a smiling figure with his hands in his lap. These figures are not meant to be worshipped. Instead, they serve as a reminder to strive for the Buddha's level of happiness and enlightenment. Bowing to a Buddha statue is meant to express thanks for his valuable lessons.

Until Westerners began visiting the Khumbu Valley in the twentieth century, the Sherpas had never climbed Mount Everest. It was considered taboo—forbidden. They believed the mountain was sacred. It was the home of gods and demons.

Although they climb Everest today, Sherpas are still very respectful of Chomolungma. They do not want to anger the Mother Goddess—they do not even like to curse on the mountain.

Before any trip to the top of Everest, a ceremony is performed in front of a stone altar. It is conducted by a spiritual leader, or lama. During the ceremony, the gods are asked to protect the climbers. The climbing equipment is also blessed. Offerings such as fruits and chocolate are placed on the altar, and fragrant juniper leaves are burned.

Prayer flags—colorful pieces of cloth with prayers written on them—are strung up.

Sherpas believe that the wind lets loose spiritual energy within the flags, sending blessings of peace and love across the land. These prayer flags can be found at the top of the mountain, too, and all around the Khumbu Valley.

Chortens can also be found on mountain trails leading up to Everest. These small stone shrines may contain offerings or smaller *mani* stones—tablets engraved with prayers. Sometimes prayer flags are found on them.

Houses of worship called monasteries also dot the landscape around Mount Everest. The largest and most famous of these is Tengboche (say: TANG-bo-chay). It is known for its beauty and its sweeping views of Mount Everest and the Himalayas. Tengboche is surrounded by *mani* stones. Prayer flags in five colors flutter in the wind.

Thousands of visitors come to Tengboche every year. Many come to take part in a special festival. It takes place over several days in the fall. Dancers in bright and colorful masks perform a series of sixteen dances. The dances show how Buddhism was first brought to Tibet.

The Sherpas are known to be a very welcoming and happy people. Because of their strength and stamina, they are an essential part of any climb on Everest. It is through recent mountain-climbing trips that many Westerners have come to know the Sherpas.

# CHAPTER 3
# The Discovery of Everest

Before the mid-1800s, hardly anyone in the Western world knew that Mount Everest even existed. Europeans and Asians traded goods with one another. However, the Himalayas were so high and rugged that all the trade routes went *around* the mountains rather than over them. And Mount Everest, standing in the center of the mountain range, was too remote to be discovered.

India had been trading spices such as black pepper, nutmeg, ginger, and cinnamon with Europe since ancient times. Then in the late 1400s, the Ottoman Empire in modern-day Turkey blocked land routes from Europe to Asia. So Europeans had to go by sea. Nothing would stop the spice trade.

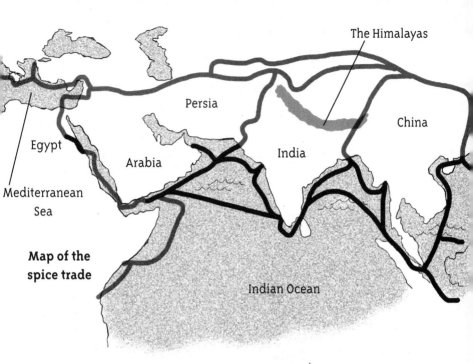

The British arrived in India in 1612 and began to set up trading posts. By the late 1700s, they controlled much of India. In 1800, they decided to map the whole region. They wanted to know exactly where places were on this part of the globe, and the distances between them.

So in 1802, a great mapping project of India began. Thousands of distances and angles were measured across India. In 1818, a young man named George Everest was hired to assist William Lambton as the Surveyor-General of India. A surveyor's job is to take measurements of land. After Lambton died, Everest was put in charge in 1830.

George Everest                    William Lambton

George Everest faced many obstacles. The instruments used for surveying were enormous. Some weighed more than one thousand pounds!

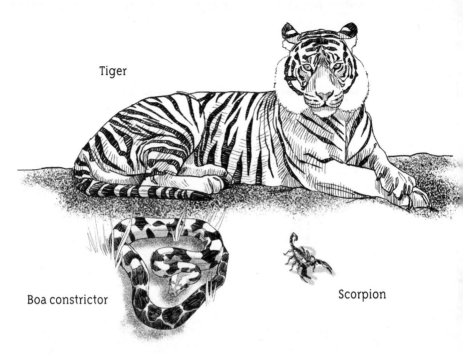

Tiger

Boa constrictor

Scorpion

They had to be carried by twelve or more men—
or by elephants. Heavy monsoon rains flooded
rivers and obscured views. So Everest had to
construct great brick towers—some as high as
fifty feet—from which to make his observations.
Survey teams worked in jungles full of tigers, boa
constrictors, and scorpions. If the animals didn't
get to the men, fever did. Many died, and more
than once Everest himself caught malaria and had
to leave India to recover.

While away from India, Everest worked to improve equipment. When he returned, he organized a team that included up to seven hundred men, dozens of camels and horses, and four elephants.

Progress was slow but steady. By 1843, when Everest retired, the survey had mapped India from its southern tip all the way to the Himalayas.

In 1847, George Everest's successor, Andrew Waugh, continued surveying the southern edge of the Himalayas. It was then that Waugh spotted a mountain he suspected to be the tallest in the world.

It took years before he could find out for sure.

Most of the year, the top of Peak XV (as it was known at the time) was covered by clouds. The mountain also lay over the border, in Nepal. The Nepalese government didn't trust the British and would not allow them to enter the country.

Waugh and his team had to make their observations from afar. The closest they got to Peak XV was 108 miles away. The information from five different places was given to human "computers." These were mathematicians who would carefully crunch the numbers to determine the height of the mountain.

Finally, in 1856, Peak XV was determined to be the tallest in the world. At the time, it was said to be 29,002 feet above sea level. There is some argument today as to the exact height—some say 29,028 feet; some 29,035. But these nineteenth-century human computers were only about one-tenth of one percent off from Peak XV's true height.

It was now more than ten years since George Everest had retired as the surveyor general. Still, Waugh decided to name the mountain after him. In 1865—one year before Everest's death—the Royal Geographic Society accepted Waugh's suggestion. Peak XV was now "Mount Everest."

# What's in a Name?

George Everest did not want the mountain named after him.

Why?

Because during the great mapping project, it had been common practice to use only names that the local people would use.

The Nepalese on Peak XV's south slope called their mountain *Sagarmatha*, or "Sky Goddess." And the Tibetans to the north—as well as the Sherpas in Nepal's Khumbu Valley—knew it as their mother goddess, Chomolungma.

George Everest respected these old names. It was for this reason that he did not wish Peak XV to be named after him. He also argued that "Everest" could not be written in Hindi, a native language of the area. Nor could the Indian people even pronounce the name. (Though its pronunciation has changed over time—Sir George's surname was actually pronounced EVE-rest.)

By this point in world history, much of the globe—the Americas, Australia, the South Pacific—had been explored and mapped. With no continents remaining to be discovered, explorers now tried to be the first to reach remote places.

In 1909, forty-four years after Mount Everest was given its name, American explorer Robert Peary reached the North Pole. Two years later,

Robert Peary
at the North Pole

Roald Amundsen
at the South Pole

Roald Amundsen and his team from Norway
made it to the South Pole. It seemed only logical
that Mount Everest—sometimes called the earth's
Third Pole—should come next . . . and the British
wanted the honor of climbing it first.

At this time, the kingdom of Nepal was closed to outsiders. That meant an approach had to be made from the north—in Tibet. Tibet, however, did not welcome foreign visitors, either. British diplomats decided to appeal to the Dalai Lama, the leader of Tibet. He gave permission to enter in 1921.

The Dalai Lama

A British team was formed. Leaving from India, they hiked more than four hundred miles into the Himalayas. For months, the team searched the valleys and glaciers along the northern and eastern sides of Mount Everest. They were hoping to find a route to the summit.

# The Golden Age of Alpinism

The first attempts to climb Mount Everest were all made by British teams.

Mountain climbing emerged as a popular sport among the British in the mid-1850s. Sir Alfred Wills, an important British judge, climbed the 12,113-foot Wetterhorn in the Swiss Alps. Wills published a book about his adventures called *Wanderings Among the High Alps*. Soon mountaineering became trendy and fashionable.

In 1857, a group of British climbers formed the Alpine Club, which still exists today. For the next few years, many peaks in the Alps were climbed for the first time. This period was known as the "golden age of Alpinism." This era ended in 1865, when the summit of the nearly fifteen-thousand-foot-high Matterhorn was reached.

# CHAPTER 4
# George Mallory

Among those on the first expedition to Everest, in 1921, was a man named George Herbert Leigh Mallory. A handsome thirty-five-year-old teacher from England, he was also an experienced mountaineer. Ten years earlier, he had climbed Mount Blanc, the tallest mountain in the Alps.

Mallory was also the man who once said he wanted to climb Everest "because it's there." He was part of the first three expeditions to the mountain.

A dozen or so Sherpas were hired to assist the British. The Sherpas did not understand why the men wanted to reach the summit of Mount Everest. In their native language, there was not even a word for *summit*!

Mallory wrote to his wife that the mountaineers were walking "off the map." They were climbing where no one ever had before. They wore many layers of clothing made from wool and silk to fight the bitter cold. Their leather boots had nails on them for gripping the icy ground.

For months, they explored the land around Everest. They climbed as high as

23,030 feet. That was higher than anyone had ever climbed before. They also produced the first good maps of the area. Violent storms and exhaustion forced an end to the expedition. But they discovered one very important thing—a route to the top!

The next year, in 1922, a new British team was formed. With maps from the first expedition in hand, they tried three times to reach the summit.

The first attempt nearly ended in disaster. One climber fell, pulling over two others, and they began to slide down a steep slope! Mallory was able to keep them from falling using his rope and ice ax.

On the second summit push, climbers reached more than 27,000 feet. But eventually the group turned back. They were simply too exhausted to continue.

Mallory led the final charge for the summit. It was June, and early snows had begun to fall. He and two British teammates, with fourteen Sherpas behind them, trudged through the waist-deep snow.

Suddenly, an avalanche surged down the mountain. Mallory and his teammates were buried. Even so, they were able to dig themselves out. However, nine of the Sherpas were swept into a deep crack, or crevasse (say: kreh-VASS). Only two survived. Mallory was terribly upset.

He blamed himself for the tragedy.

The third expedition to Everest in 1924 would be Mallory's last. A freak storm plunged temperatures to nearly forty degrees below zero. That's cold enough to freeze human skin within minutes.

Mallory wrote to his wife that the trip had "been a bad time altogether." He said he was "looking out of a tent door on to a world of snow and vanishing hopes."

On the morning of June 8, Mallory set off for the summit with Andrew Irvine. He was Mallory's twenty-two-year-old climbing partner. They were last spotted at 12:50 in the afternoon—two small black dots nearing the top of the mountain. Suddenly, clouds blew in and covered them. It was as if they had disappeared. Shortly after, a snowstorm kicked up. It became clear after a few days that both men had died.

It took almost seventy-five years before Mallory's frozen body was discovered. It is believed that he fell to his death while roped to Andrew Irvine. However, his partner's body has never been found. Some believe Mallory may have reached the summit of Mount Everest before his death. But no one can know for sure.

# CHAPTER 5
## The Swiss Take a Turn

After the tragedies of 1922 and 1924, the Dalai Lama decided to close Tibet's borders again. No further attempts were allowed on Everest for nearly a decade.

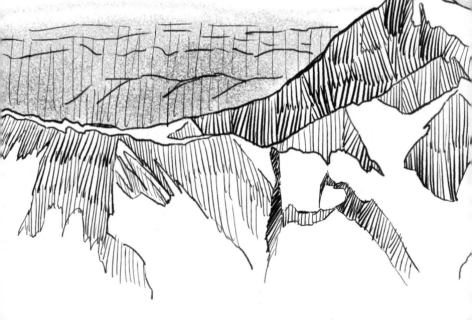

The British goal of reaching the summit did not die, however. In the 1930s, airplanes were able to fly around the mountain, revealing more possible routes.

In 1933, Frank Smythe attempted to reach the summit alone. He reached an altitude of 28,200 feet before turning around due to fatigue. Smythe said that while climbing, he saw mirages. A mirage is when you see something and your mind thinks it is real, but it's not.

In Smythe's mirage, he had a climbing partner with him, and the two were connected by a rope. He thought that if he slipped, his friend would save him.

Smythe also thought he saw two dark objects floating in the sky. One, he said, looked like a kite-balloon. The other looked like it had small wings and a beak. They both appeared to vibrate, he said, before vanishing behind some clouds. Was any of this real? There is no way to know.

Due to illness, accidents, and poor weather conditions, other expeditions in the 1930s—all by British teams—failed to reach the top. When World War II erupted in Europe in 1939, attempts to climb Everest were put on hold. After the war, the Chinese government took over Tibet and closed the region's borders. Approaching Mount Everest from the north was no longer an option.

Around this same time, India became independent from Great Britain. With the British gone, Nepal finally opened its borders. A southern approach to the summit was now possible. But it meant being brave enough to climb the treacherous Khumbu Icefall.

# The Khumbu Icefall

The Khumbu Icefall sits at the top of the Khumbu Glacier, which is the highest glacier in the world. A glacier is a slow-moving area of ice, and an icefall—like a waterfall—is where this frozen water "falls" down a wall of rocks.

The Khumbu Icefall moves down the slopes of Everest as much as four feet every day. As it moves, it opens up wide, deep crevasses. It also breaks the glacial ice into towering seracs. Seracs are apartment building—size blocks of ice that can crash down without warning. The deadly accident on April 18, 2014, was the result of a falling serac.

On his first trip to Everest in 1921, George Mallory spotted the Khumbu Icefall from afar. He said it looked "terribly steep and broken." Mallory considered it impossible to climb. But it was through the icefall that the first successful trip to the summit—and many to follow—was taken.

In 1951, a British team nearly made it through the icefall, before a hundred-foot-wide crevasse put an end to the climb.

The next year, the Nepalese government let a Swiss group go up the mountain. They climbed the Khumbu Icefall in five days. The team went down sixty feet into the crevasse that had stopped the British the year before. They found a snow bridge partway across, then installed a shaky rope ladder to complete the trip to the other side.

# The Yeti

The yeti is a creature of legend similar to Bigfoot in North America. With long, shaggy hair, the apelike yeti is believed by some to inhabit the snowy Himalayas.

A 1951 expedition brought news of the yeti! Thirteen-inch "footprints" were photographed on a snowy slope. The pictures appeared in a London newspaper. Later it was revealed to be a practical joke.

After crossing the icefall, the Swiss entered the Western Cwm (say: KOOM). The Cwm is a deep, bowl-shaped valley. The Western Cwm—sometimes called the Valley of Silence— is surrounded by snow-covered mountainsides. When sunlight reflects off the white snow on windless days, temperatures can climb as high as ninety-five degrees!

Next for the Swiss came the Lhotse Face. The fourth-tallest mountain in the world, Lhotse (say: lote-SAY) is connected to Everest by a high, rocky field called the South Col.

From the South Col, a Sherpa and the Swiss leader made a push for Everest's summit. They went along Everest's Southeast Ridge. They set a climbing record of 28,199 feet. That was when their oxygen tanks stopped working. There was no choice but to turn around just short of the top.

In thirty-one years, no one had reached the top of Mount Everest. Getting there always seemed beyond reach. But the next year, 1953, everything changed.

# CHAPTER 6
# Hillary and Tenzing

In 1953, Edmund Hillary and Tenzing Norgay grabbed the prize: They became the first men to reach the summit of Everest. Although they came from very different places, they became trusted friends and partners.

Edmund Hillary was born in Auckland, New Zealand, on July 20, 1919. When he was sixteen, Edmund went on a field trip to the tallest mountain on New Zealand's North Island. Though he was uncoordinated, Edmund discovered he was stronger than his

Edmund Hillary

companions. Mountain climbing became a lifelong hobby. Hillary served in the Royal New Zealand Air Force during World War II and raised bees for a living with his brother, Rex.

Tenzing Norgay was born in May 1914 in the Khumbu Valley. The eleventh of thirteen children, Tenzing grew up in the shadow of Mount Everest in the village of Tengboche. He was sent to the famous Tengboche Monastery to become a monk, but Tenzing decided that wasn't for him. When he was twenty, Tenzing joined an expedition to Everest as a porter. A porter's job is to carry supplies up and down the mountain. He joined other climbs during the 1930s. In time, Tenzing became the most trusted Sherpa guide on Everest.

Tenzing Norgay

Thirty-three-year-old Edmund Hillary and thirty-nine-year-old Tenzing Norgay joined the 1953 British expedition to Everest. It was a massive operation. Ten tons of food and equipment were carried by more than 350 porters, twenty guides, and ten climbers. Tenzing was the leader of the Sherpa guides. It was his seventh trip up the mountain.

Not everyone in the group would try to reach the summit. John Hunt, the expedition leader, had to see how everyone performed first. In the end, he chose two pairs of climbers to make the final trip. Small teams of Sherpas and "support climbers" would carry supplies up the mountain. They would help the summit climbers set up their camps before returning to lower altitudes to sleep at their own camps.

John Hunt

The expedition went through the icefall and the Western Cwm. The men climbed up the Lhotse Face to the South Col. From there, Tom Bourdillon and Charles Evans, the first pair, attempted a summit push on May 26. They reached the South Summit at 28,750 feet. They were less than three hundred feet from the tip-top of the mountain. But their oxygen tanks were acting up, and the men were exhausted. Bourdillon and Evans returned to camp, defeated but alive.

Three days later, the second pair of climbers—Hillary and Tenzing—tried to reach the top. After a cold and windy night camped at 27,900 feet, they awoke at four in the morning. The day was clear. Tenzing whooped in delight when he spotted Tengboche Monastery miles below. For Tenzing, that was a good sign from the gods.

Tenzing and Hillary ate a breakfast of sardines on crackers. They also drank plenty of lemon juice with sugar to fight off weakness. Hillary's boots had gotten wet the day before, and were frozen solid. For two hours, he cooked the boots over their campfire, drying them and softening up the leather.

At 6:30, they set out wearing heavy parkas, breathing masks, and thirty pounds of oxygen gear. Tenzing wore boots made of reindeer fur. They hiked to the South Summit, where their friends had had to turn around days earlier.

The two made good time. They continued to the Cornice Traverse, a frightening path of rock and snow. Using ice axes, Hillary and Tenzing cut away footholds to walk in. One careful step at a time, the two crossed the narrow knife-edge of snow. Any misstep to the left or right would send them falling to their deaths, a mile and a half below.

Suddenly they came to a forty-foot-high wall of rock and snow. The rock was smooth and appeared to have no footholds. How could they get up it? All at once, Hillary spotted ice running along a crack in

the rock. He backed his body into the crack. Then he kicked backward, sinking the spiky metal teeth on the bottom of his boots, called crampons, into the ice behind him. Bit by bit, using his crampons, he worked his way up the rock.

After reaching the top, Edmund lay on his back to catch his breath. He helped pull Tenzing Norgay up the rock.

Finally, the summit was within sight!

The two men walked another couple hundred feet on the snowy dome. At 11:30 in the morning on May 29, 1953, the summit of Mount Everest was reached! Overjoyed, the men hugged each other.

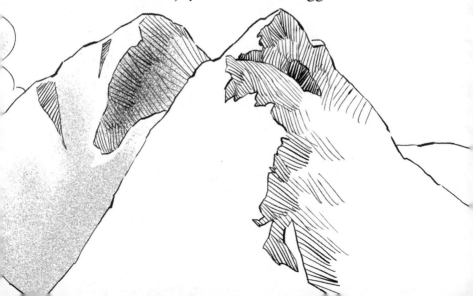

Holding the flags of Great Britain, Nepal, India, and the United Nations, Tenzing Norgay posed for a picture.

But there was little time for celebration. They were running low on oxygen. Tenzing buried an offering of crackers and sweets to the gods. Hillary placed a cross in the snow. After just fifteen minutes on top of the world, the two began their descent.

News of Hillary and Tenzing's success reached Great Britain a few days later, on June 2. It was the same day Elizabeth II was crowned queen of England. It was a day of true excitement and celebration. The media called the conquering of Mount Everest a gift for the new monarch.

For his achievements, Tenzing Norgay was awarded medals by the queen, and by the nations of India and Nepal. He was treated as a god among his people. Later on, he went on to start a mountain-climbing company. In 1996, ten years after his death, Tenzing's son Jamling followed in his father's footsteps and reached the top of Everest.

Edmund was knighted by the new queen. That meant from then on he was known as *Sir* Edmund Hillary. Having conquered the earth's Third Pole, he later went on to reach both the North and South Poles. He was the first man in the world to reach both poles and summit Everest. In 1990, his son, Peter, climbed Mount Everest, making them the first father and son to achieve the summit. Edmund dedicated his life to improving the lives of the Sherpa people. He built schools, clinics, and hospitals. He became known as the "Godfather of Khumbu."

Peter Hillary

# Everest Expeditions Since 1953

The first Americans to reach the summit of Everest did so in 1963. James Whittaker, with Sherpa Nawang Gombu, reached the summit on May 1, following the path of Hillary and Tenzing. Three weeks later, Willi Unsoeld and Tom Hornbein also followed that path, climbing through the icefall to the Western Cwm. But rather than climb the Lhotse Face, they climbed to the Western Ridge. This was a much more difficult path to take, and they were the first to do it.

Junko Tabei of Japan became the first woman to climb Everest, in 1975. In 1978, an Italian and an Austrian were the first to climb without oxygen tanks. And in 1980, a Polish team was the first to reach the top during the wintertime. They faced winds of one hundred miles per hour and temperatures close to fifty degrees below zero!

In 1970, Yuichiro Miura became the first man to *ski* down Mount Everest! Miura skied more than 6,500 feet down the mountain, then fell for 1,300 feet along the rocky Lhotse Face. He used a large parachute to slow his descent, and stopped just 250 feet from the edge of a crevasse! A film about him, *The Man Who Skied Down Everest*, won an Academy Award.

# CHAPTER 7
## The Death Zone

Falling ice and avalanches are not the only risks when climbing Mount Everest. Climbing at high altitudes can have dangerous, even deadly, effects on the human body.

The higher up the mountain, the harder it becomes to breathe. That's because oxygen is more scattered—more spread out. A person near the top of Everest breathes in only about a third as much oxygen as they would at sea level. The air is so "thin" that the body must fight for every bit of oxygen it can get. The less oxygen the body receives, the more dangerous climbing becomes.

Above the Khumbu Icefall and the Western Cwm—26,000 feet up—lies Mount Everest's Death Zone. In the Death Zone, the air is so thin that unless climbers breathe from oxygen tanks, most will faint within minutes. Some even die. Nothing can survive for too long in the Death Zone.

Death Zone

Even below the Death Zone, climbers can experience a danger known as altitude sickness. Symptoms include headache, loss of appetite, nausea, irritability, and dizziness. In more serious cases, fluid fills the lungs and makes a person cough up bubbly pink mucus.

In the worst form of altitude sickness, the brain swells with fluid. This can lead to vomiting and blindness. Parts of the body can become paralyzed. Climbers become confused, forgetting where they are and the dangers they face. Some people have been known to remove their oxygen tanks or layers of protective clothing—or even wander off alone, never to be seen again.

Climbers with severe altitude sickness must be brought to down to lower elevations. If they are not treated right away, they may die. But rescue operations are difficult on Everest. Helicopters can fly only in good weather. Also, the air is so thin that the helicopter blades have little to "grab" on to. Landing a helicopter on Everest is dangerous.

## Surviving in Thin Air

There are ways to lower the risk of altitude sickness. A person's body can adjust to surviving on less oxygen. It is important to climb a mountain slowly, and to spend time at various altitudes. This gives the body a chance to get used to its new surroundings. The lungs breathe faster, working hard to bring in as much oxygen as possible. More red blood cells are produced to carry oxygen to different parts of the body.

It can take two months for the body to become used to life on Everest. Today, just below the Khumbu Icefall lies Everest Base Camp. Here, climbers will camp out for weeks, so their bodies can adjust to the high altitude. Most guides then take climbers up and down a portion of the mountain a number of times before allowing anyone to enter the Death Zone. After spending time at various camps on the mountain, climbers typically return to Base Camp to regain their strength before making the final trip to the summit.

The severe weather on Everest can also be a killer. Exposure to extreme cold and wind can lower the body's temperature to dangerous levels where the heart and lungs can no longer work.

Frostbite occurs when a person's skin is exposed to extremely cold air. The blood vessels around the exposed skin shrink. When this happens, blood can no longer flow to the area.

Frostbite most often hits the fingers, nose, ears, and toes. The frozen skin goes numb, and sometimes dies. The skin hardens and turns black. In bad cases of frostbite, toes or fingers must be amputated, or cut off.

# Treating Frostbite

When people are out in extremely cold weather, they often wiggle their fingers and toes. This improves blood circulation and helps prevent frostbite. When people can't feel their fingers or toes, it can be an early sign of frostbite. Frostbite can occur in as little as five minutes.

When a person develops frostbite, the most important thing is to thaw the affected area right away. For example, you can put frostbitten fingers into a bowl of warm water and gradually heat the water up. Once the tissue is thawed, the area must be kept warm and not exposed to the cold. Direct heat from fires or heating pads is not advised, nor should the skin be rubbed or massaged. Often there is no lasting damage from frostbite.

## Wildlife Near the Death Zone

Although no creatures can survive in Everest's Death Zone, many can live at slightly lower elevations.

The Himalayan jumping spider has been spotted on Everest as high  as 22,000 feet. This tiny spider feeds on the frozen bodies of flies and other insects that have been carried up by the winds from lower altitudes.

Yaks can survive at 20,000 feet, feeding on mosses that grow high up the mountain. The yellow-billed chough is a species of bird similar to a crow. It has been spotted as high as the South Col. That's nearly 26,000 feet up.

It hunts for food (sometimes human bodies!) left behind by climbing expeditions.

Farther down the mountain live mountain goats, Himalayan wolves, and the snow leopard.

# CHAPTER 8
## Mount Everest Today

Climbing Mount Everest today is very different from the days of George Mallory and Edmund Hillary. Before 1951, Nepal, Tibet, and China allowed only one expedition to climb the mountain every year. Even after 1951, the number of climbers was strictly limited.

But people around the world wanted to follow in Hillary's and Tenzing's footsteps. In time, Nepal and China let anybody try who had the money.

Every year since 1998, more than one hundred people have reached the top of Everest. In 2000, it was 145 people. By 2010, it was 536! This has led to deadly traffic jams on the mountain.

In 1996, eight people died when a blizzard suddenly appeared on the summit. Among them was a famous guide named Rob Hall. At the time, he had climbed Everest more times than any non-Sherpa in the world. Seven more would die on the mountain that season.

On May 18, 2012, two hundred climbers, accompanied by more than two hundred guides, attempted to reach the summit on the same day.

A storm was due the next day, so everyone tried to reach the summit early. With only one route up to the top, people stood single-file for hours, shivering and suffering from altitude sickness. In the end, 234 reached the top, but four people died.

## Trash at the Top of the World

The increased traffic on Mount Everest has led to another problem: garbage. The slopes of Everest are now littered with piles of empty oxygen tanks, broken tents, sleeping bags—even dead bodies.

But efforts are being made to clean up Mount Everest. Sherpas receive a reward for any oxygen tanks they return. And the Nepalese government now requires every climber to bring back eighteen pounds of garbage.

Although climbing Everest is by no means easy, lighter equipment, better weather forecasting, and experienced Sherpas have increased the odds of reaching the summit. In 1990, only 18 percent of summit attempts were successful. By 2013, it was 64 percent. People as young as thirteen—and as old as eighty—have made it to the top.

Malavath Poorna climbed Everest when she was just thirteen.

Climbers today follow a fixed route, holding ropes that are set in place before the climb starts. They cross the crevasses of the Khumbu Icefall on sturdy aluminum ladders. These ropes and ladders are installed early in the season by Sherpas.

The Sherpas who died on the Khumbu Icefall in 2014 were on the mountain early in the season, setting the course for that year's climbers.

There is little chance that traffic on Mount Everest will slow down. Nepal charges $25,000 for a permit to climb the mountain. For such a poor country, this money is sorely needed.

After paying for a permit, people who wish to climb Everest often hire

guides and Sherpas. Climbers spend anywhere from $10,000 to $100,000 in their attempts to reach the top.

The Sherpa community relies on this money. A Sherpa guide can expect to make between $2,000 and $8,000 in one season. With most people in Nepal making $600 or $700 a year, this is a huge sum. The money makes it worth the risks.

And the risks are many.

Because the Sherpas carry supplies to and from camps along the slopes, they cross the Khumbu Icefall dozens of times every season. This increases the chances of deadly accidents.

After the horrible day in April 2014, the Nepalese government offered each of the victims' families only $400. This small amount made the Sherpa community furious. They went on strike, ending the climbing season for the year.

# Climate Change

Temperatures in the Himalayas have risen 0.5 degrees Fahrenheit every decade since 1980. The Khumbu Glacier has shrunk by more than half a mile over the past fifty years. It is possible that climate change could be to blame for the recent deadly accident on the icefall. The icefall has been moving a few feet down the mountain every day for years, with cracks forming often. Some experts say that, with the glacial ice melting faster and faster, the Khumbu Icefall is more unstable than ever.

Despite the dangers and the Sherpa strike of 2014, people continue to visit Mount Everest.

Since ancient times, humans have pushed themselves to the limit—to the ends of the earth. We looked at the sea and imagined faraway lands full of riches. We built great ships, crossing thousands of miles of ocean to reach every corner of the globe. We gazed at the sky and became determined to reach the moon.

By the time Edmund Hillary and Tenzing Norgay climbed Everest, scientists in the United States and Russia were already planning travel into space. But while Neil Armstrong walked on the moon just sixteen years later, in 1969, it was two men—a beekeeper from New Zealand and a Sherpa from Nepal—who first stood on the earth from above, high atop Chomolungma, Mother Goddess of the World.

# Timeline of Mount Everest

| | |
|---|---|
| c. 80,000,000 BC | India, an island at this time, begins to drift toward Asia |
| c. 50,000,000 BC | India crashes into Asia; Himalayas begin to form |
| 1533 | Khumbu Valley settled |
| 1802 | British begin great mapping project of India |
| 1830 | George Everest becomes surveyor general of the Great Trigonometrical Survey of India |
| 1847 | Everest's successor, Andrew Waugh, spots Peak XV |
| 1856 | Peak XV declared the tallest mountain in the world |
| 1865 | Peak XV named Mount Everest |
| 1921 | First British expedition to Everest |
| 1924 | Third British expedition to Everest; George Mallory dies |
| 1952 | Swiss expedition crosses the Khumbu Icefall |
| 1953 | Edmund Hillary and Tenzing Norgay reach the summit of Mount Everest |
| 1975 | Junko Tabei of Japan becomes the first woman to climb Everest |
| 1993 | China and Nepal greatly reduce restrictions on climbing Everest; forty climbers reach the summit on a single day |
| 1996 | Eight people lose their lives on Everest in the deadliest climbing season to date |
| 2012 | A traffic jam of four hundred people on Everest leads to the death of four |
| 2014 | Sixteen Sherpas die on the Khumbu Icefall on the deadliest day in Mount Everest's history |

# Timeline of the World

| | |
|---|---|
| The dinosaurs become extinct | c. 65,000,000 BC |
| Leonardo da Vinci paints the *Mona Lisa* | 1503-1506 |
| St. Augustine, the oldest city in the United States, is founded | 1565 |
| Louisiana Purchase doubles the size of the United States | 1803 |
| Photography is invented | 1826 |
| United States declares war on Mexico; annexes California and New Mexico two years later | 1846 |
| Harriet Beecher Stowe's antislavery book *Uncle Tom's Cabin* is published | 1852 |
| Civil War in the United States ends | 1865 |
| Nineteenth Amendment to the Constitution ratified, giving women in the United States the right to vote | 1920 |
| Color television introduced in the United States | 1951 |
| Six-Day War is fought between Israel and its Arab neighbors | 1967 |
| Nelson Mandela elected president of South Africa | 1994 |
| O.J. Simpson trial begins in the United States | 1995 |
| Barack Obama elected president of the United States | 2008 |
| Benedict XVI becomes the first pope to resign in nearly seven hundred years | 2013 |

# Bibliography

Astbury, Louise, director. *How the Earth Was Made: Everest.* New York:
    A&E Television Networks, 2010.

Browne, David. **"Everest's Deadly Traffic Jam."** *Men's Journal*, August
    2012.

Clark, Liesl, director. *Everest: 50 Years on the Mountain.* DVD.
    Washington, DC: National Geographic Society, 2003.

Coburn, Broughton. *Everest: Mountain without Mercy.* Washington,
    DC: National Geographic Society, 1997.

Gillman, Peter, ed. *Everest: The Best Writing and Pictures from
    Seventy Years of Human Endeavour.* London: Little, Brown and
    Company, 1993.

Gurubacharya, Binaj. **"Mount Everest Avalanche Is Deadliest Incident
    Ever at World's Highest Peak."** Associated Press, April 17, 2014.

Kelly, Jon. **"Everest Crowds: The World's Highest Traffic Jam."** *BBC News Magazine*, May 28, 2013.

Krakauer, Jon. **"Death and Anger on Everest."** *The New Yorker*, April 21, 2014.

Krakauer, Jon. *Into Thin Air: A Personal Account of the Mt. Everest Disaster.* New York: Villard Books, 1997.

Narula, Svati Kirsten. **"The Year Climate Change Closed Everest."** *The Atlantic*, April 28, 2014. http://www.theatlantic.com/international/archive/2014/04/the-year-climate-change-closed-everest/361114/.

Ortner, Sherry B. *High Religion: A Cultural and Political History of Sherpa Buddhism.* Princeton, NJ: Princeton University Press, 1989.

Reid, Chip. **"Climbing Mount Everest: Once Lonely, Now Crowded, But Always Treacherous."** CBS News, April 18, 2014.

first person to read
this copy! yay!
— BOB

Deez!
Nuts!
got eee...